Sanford Hirsch
Painted Sculptures

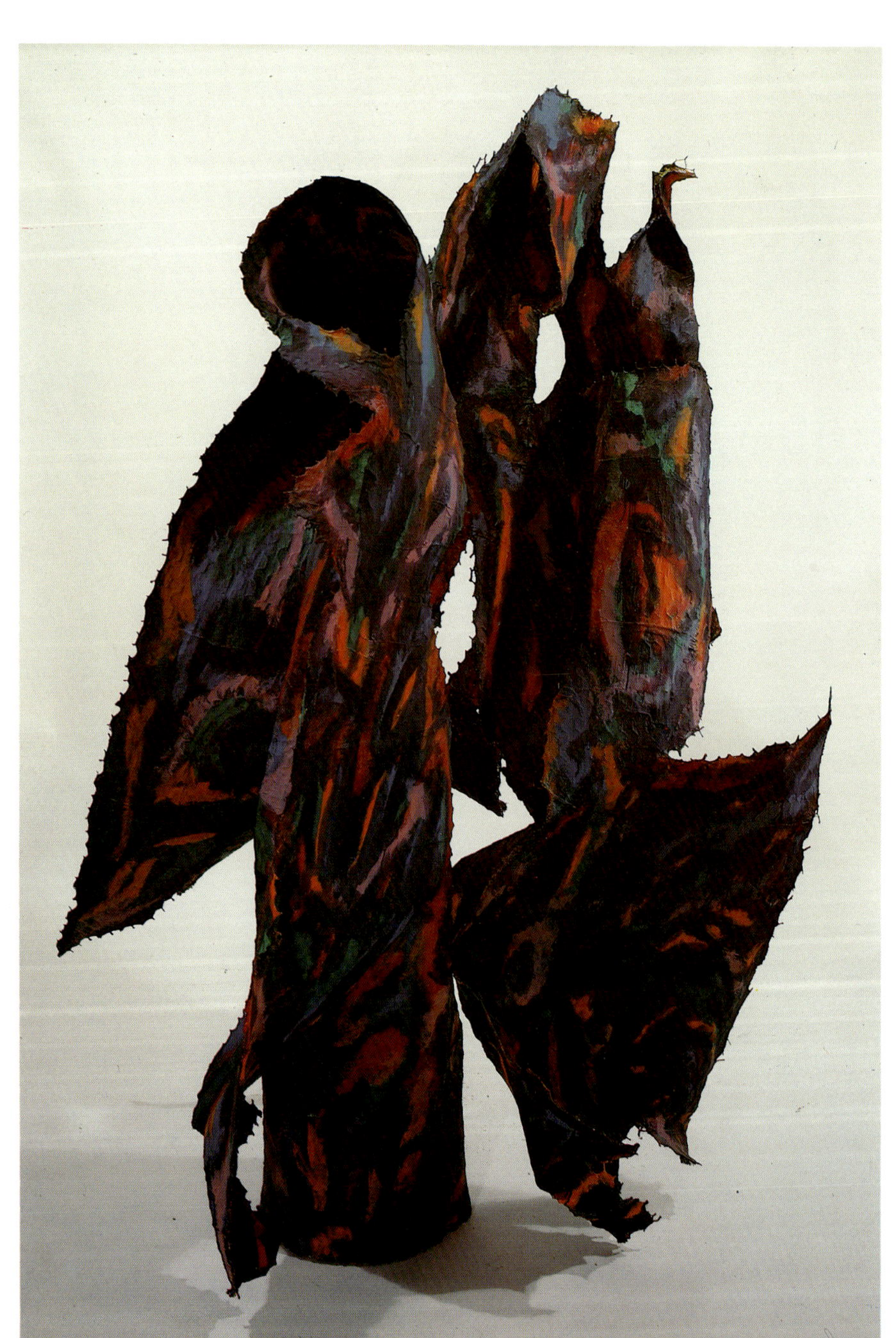

Sanford Hirsch
Painted Sculptures

Ball State University Art Gallery
Flint Institute of Arts

1985

This catalogue was published on the occasion of the exhibition *Sanford Hirsch Painted Sculptures* organized jointly by the Ball State University Art Gallery and the Flint Institute of Arts. We are grateful to the artist for his assistance with the project and to the staffs of both institutions for their vital contributions to the exhibition. The photographs that appear here were provided by Peter Muscato. This publication was made possible in part by a grant from the Institute of Museum Services, a federal agency that offers general operating support to the nation's museums.

Ball State University Art Gallery
Muncie, Indiana
December 15, 1985–January 19, 1986

Flint Institute of Arts
Flint, Michigan
February 2–March 16, 1986

Cover:
Old Bones, 1985
Catalogue no. 10

Frontispiece:
Manifest, 1983
Catalogue no. 8

Introduction

The three-dimensional painted structures of Sanford Hirsch express rugged power. Their vigorous irregularity of shape, texture, and color endow them with forceful individuality. Both free-standing and wall-hanging, these constructions embody an experimental bringing together of separate media, enhanced by textured surfaces that are coordinated so that their physical makeup and exploration of color are merged into an architectonic form.

> I start with a fairly vague idea that will not simply be for a shape—there is some color idea or some emotional idea that I will work around. The shapes will develop as I am building each piece. The physical structure will continue to evolve up until the point that the work is finished. Sometimes, even after they are painted, I will add or subtract fragments to make the shapes more specific. The process becomes a unified one; it is not a matter of doing either the painting or the sculpture.[1]

Hirsch described the technical process by which the sculptures are fabricated as follows:

> I first work with the wire and build a structure to help me develop the form. There are certain things that the structure can and cannot do and that is part of the fun—forcing it to do what it doesn't want to do. This framework is covered with gessoed cheesecloth which gives it solidity. At every stage of building, the forms are being sculpturally adjusted by cutting, adding, or subtracting shapes. Even while they are being painted, essentially I am doing the two together [painting and sculpture] because the forms are changing throughout the process. I do not consider them as two distinct functions that have a division where one ends and the other begins.[2]

The broad strokes of rich color create a multilayered patina that affects the concave and convex spatial surfaces of the three-dimensional object, modifying the individual projections and recesses. In this fashion the artist consciously relies upon color as his primary means of imparting to the sculptures a sense of weight. It is as if the geometry of Tatlin's constructions were integrated with the ornamental and often color-encrusted shapes of Gaudi's asymmetrical visionary permutations on the Gothic.

Hirsch's intensely variegated color constructions stimulate a wealth of associations with both natural phenomena and his predecessors in the traditions: modern, ancient, and non-western. The artist has drawn upon each, freely and intelligently, within the new context of his own perceptions. Approached from any vantage point, a seven-foot work such as *Manifest* (Frontispiece, catalogue no. 8) of 1983 conveys a sense of mountainous crags, mysterious concavities with multicolored projected formations that reverberate a somber, inferno-like color surface. One feels an awareness of Soutine's *Carcass of Beef*,[3] itself a variation upon Rembrandt's earlier painting of the same subject. Soutine, of course, applies his color layers on a two-dimensional surface, creating an energetic thrust and counterthrust in space that are the primary motifs of his composition. Hirsch's three-dimensional adaptation of this theme of var-icolored motion in space further removes it from an illustrative source, just as Soutine had transformed Rembrandt's image. He endows his work with a power evocative of the weathered, eroded rock formations of the American Southwest. His thick, scumbled incrusta-tions of paint tend, unlike the juiciness and saturation of Soutines's textures, toward the ab-stract and the relatively matte color effects of an artist like Clifford Still. Hirsch's surfaces avoid the intimate bejeweled sparkle and sidestep the internal glow and transparency com-mon to many paintings in favor of austere, dry effects that fuse the reticulating volumes, whether they stand free in space or jut forth from the wall in horizontal drama.

In works like *Lifeline* (catalogue no. 9) of 1984 and *Old Bones* (cover plate, catalogue no. 10) of 1985, profiles become even more dramatic, almost flamelike, and their color harmonies more forceful. In many instances, Hirsch is inspired by the vibrant coated surfaces of African and Oceanic painted sculpture, textiles, and, perhaps most important, the striking body painting—in which the body itself is treated as a three-dimensional object to be ornamented—which is a pervasive feature of many of these tribal cultures.[4] The often bizarre three-dimensional shapes underscore the sense of the constructions as mysterious, even talis-manic, objects as in the work of Ernst, Giacometti, or African and Oceanic tribal traditions. Picasso's small-scale painted bronze, *Glass of Absinthe*[5], of 1914 or David Smith's later, large-scale painted sculptures seem to have been an inspiration and point of departure for Hirsch's approach to his free-standing constructions. At times the work assumes a color character resembling camouflage, and all have qualities recalling cacti or other desert plant forms. The striking color relations in each of these constructions bespeak a direct, emotional, almost con-frontational engagement on the part of the artist.

The works on display, created over a period of eight years, extend from the relatively sim-ple monochromatic wall pieces of 1978 and 1979 (catalogue nos. 1 and 2) to such recent com-plex organizations of color and space as *Lifeline* and *Old Bones*. Hirsch's development and continuing experimentation reflect the involvement of some young American artists with the problems bequeathed to them by earlier twentieth-century pioneers. Attempting to make something rationally whole of the innovations of the preceding generations of artists by con-solidating the pictorial and the sculptural is a creative extension of their explorations. As ex-emplified by the artist's statement included here, Hirsch has a firm awareness of what artists who preceded him were striving for and of the values that their work represents to the con-temporary era. As he continues to forge his own values and to perfect the expressive means to give them substance, we can both enjoy and learn from his progress as we anticipate the results of experiments yet to come.

Alain G. Joyaux
Director
Ball State University Art Gallery

Richard J. Wattenmaker
Director
Flint Institute of Arts

Notes

[1]Interview with the artist, September 1985.
[2]Ibid.
[3]Albright-Knox Art Gallery, Buffalo (oil on canvas, 55¼ × 42 ⅜ inches, circa 1925). The artist executed a number of variations of this composition.
[4]See, e.g., Cole, Herbert M. and Ross, Doran H. The Arts of Ghana, Los Angeles: The University of California Press, 1977.
[5]The Museum of Modern Art, Gift of Mrs. Bertram Smith (8¾ inches high).

Artist's Statement

Sanford Hirsch
born Jersey City, New Jersey, June 17, 1951
resides in New York City

The artist's statement was transcribed and edited from a February 1985 presentation at Drew University, Madison, New Jersey. Additional comments were excerpted from an interview with the artist conducted by Alain G. Joyaux and Richard J. Wattenmaker in September 1985.

I use the word *sculpture* as a convenience, to explain that the work I do is three-dimensional. The traditional uses of the terms *painting* and *sculpture* always seemed out of date to me; their currency was ended sometime in the late 1950s. In the objects that I make, I do use many of the elements of both approaches to making art. There is no escaping dealing with issues of structure and form when building anything; and to the extent that I want to proceed beyond the usual expectations of the physical shape, I can see no better or more highly evolved means to use than those of painting.

Painted objects and painted sculptures are nothing new. Most ancient cultures painted their statuary as well as their architecture. Color on an object is of primary importance to most tribal cultures. In my work I try to deal with some of the same basic ideas as these other kinds of societies. This way of working extends from a basic feeling about the reality of things; in my case it includes the reality of art and the artist. The impact conveyed by a form which has color and pose is close to that of encountering another person or animal. It immediately raises physical and emotional awareness to consider the approach of something real. It tells the viewer to be alert and to some extent to be wary.

Part of the impact of sculpture today is in its confrontational nature. The ability to utilize forms in a way that will both draw people in and hold them off is crucial to my work. That these qualities can be enhanced through the painting of the works is also critical. Our reactions to paint and a painted surface are as strong as our reactions to form. In my work, the confrontational nature of the object forces one to look at or look away from the painted surface. I don't want to imply that there's a division between surface and form, but that there is a specific relationship that comes into play. This process dictates that the nature of the painting needs to be specific to each form.

That this happens is a result of the types of forms that I use as well as my feelings about painting. The forms are specific and unplanned; there are no studies or drawings prepared. They are the result of a process of building, evaluating, and more building. Since I become involved in this process, the forms have much to do with my own physical relationship to the structure. The results are complex and unsimplified. There is no back or front, all orientations are equally important. Interior and exterior surfaces are interconnected and exist concurrently. The painting, therefore, has to function similarly to and equal this impact in order to have any substance. It becomes a second complete process of consideration and work.

Prior to 1972, I painted on material that was stretched not on stretchers but out in actual space, and used color in these looser forms. From there I tried to work with the structure, and I began to feel that I wanted to get a very solid concentrated object which resulted, ultimately, in works like the two wall works (catalogue nos. 1 and 2). From the wall works I became more and more interested in free-standing objects, and this led me to a whole other series of problems and concerns that centered on the question of how to deal with the real sculptural qualities of the work, the color and the level of intensity that I wanted to use to achieve a unified meaningful object.

In order to convey the emotional realities which are my goal, it's important not simply to make painted sculptures, but to create entire objects with their own internal logic and rationale. It's not important for me to make a structure and then highlight certain areas by painting them. The specifics of the painting on these objects are too critical to their success or failure. Therefore, it is important to use different techniques, types of paint and color, and ways of applying the color. The nuances of the painting are enhanced by the physicality of the object, thereby posing more of a challenge for me and for the viewer.

I find, lately, I am drawn more and more toward architectural structures and environments. One thing that comes to mind is my visit in 1983 to the Dome of the Rock in Jerusalem. The building was so unlike anything I had ever seen or been in or been near that it radically changed the way I am able to consider space and objects, light and color.

Color is always important, and I am constantly learning more about how to use it more directly. The problem is using color in this way on a physical form rather than delineating areas of the form or painting the entire form one or two colors. For a while I was working with the idea of color against the idea of form. I was making the structures very solid and very strong in order to see if I could have the color—when I say *color* I mean tonality, surface, and all the qualities of paint and color—be equally strong and have both work together. Now, I feel more comfortable with my own abilities so that I can go back to using more subtle approaches in putting on color.

In dealing with the objects, there is a sense of scale that comes into play. This exists not so much in absolute size, that is large or small, but in a need to work against the contemporary idea of heroics in art. Much of contemporary art has built itself on an idea of heroic scale— we've come to regard monumentality as an integral value in the visual arts. While less may or may not have been more, bigger is regarded as more serious. That this idea is overly simplistic should be obvious, yet the trend continues. In my work I need to limit myself to my own scale both to keep myself on track and to try to change what I regard as a dehumanizing trend.

During the process of painting, which is similar to the building process, the forms, in a sense, dictate their colors and surfaces. The result is an object that is important in how it affects someone. There is no attempt in this work to deal with symbols or narrative. The reality of the object that has been made must communicate something of my reality directly to the viewer as he or she is exposed to it.

The key for me is to be able to respond freely to my instincts and accept the fact that I've spent a long time looking closely at many kinds of painting and sculpture. I can't claim ignorance of formal criteria, only an interest in following my own intuition despite what I've seen or read.

I started out as a musician several years ago. Concentrating on the emotional rather than the intellectual aspects of making the work remains very important to me. The idea of flow; the idea of developing the work out of the work; of making a whole and having it evolve out of myself and really forcing myself to do that; using techniques that I've learned, that I've developed so that I can continue to learn and develop. If you're a performer you have to be current. To be an artist you have to deal with what you know and what you allow yourself to do and that's all. If you can push yourself to that limit you're not only current, you're ahead of it and that's what making art is about. The challenge to yourself and your ability to meet that challenge are what count in the long run.

Catalogue of the Exhibition

1. *Untitled*, 1978
   tempera and lacquer over gessoed fabric
     and wire
   74 × 10 × 5 inches

2. *Unflap*, 1979
   lacquer over gessoed fabric and wire
   49 × 15½ × 6 inches

3. *To Hold Onto*, 1981
   oil, tempera, and enamel over gessoed fabric
     and wire
   30 × 52 × 26 inches
   illustrated

4. *Untitled*, 1981
   oil and enamel over gessoed fabric and wire
   27 × 49 × 12½ inches

To Hold Onto, catalogue no. 3

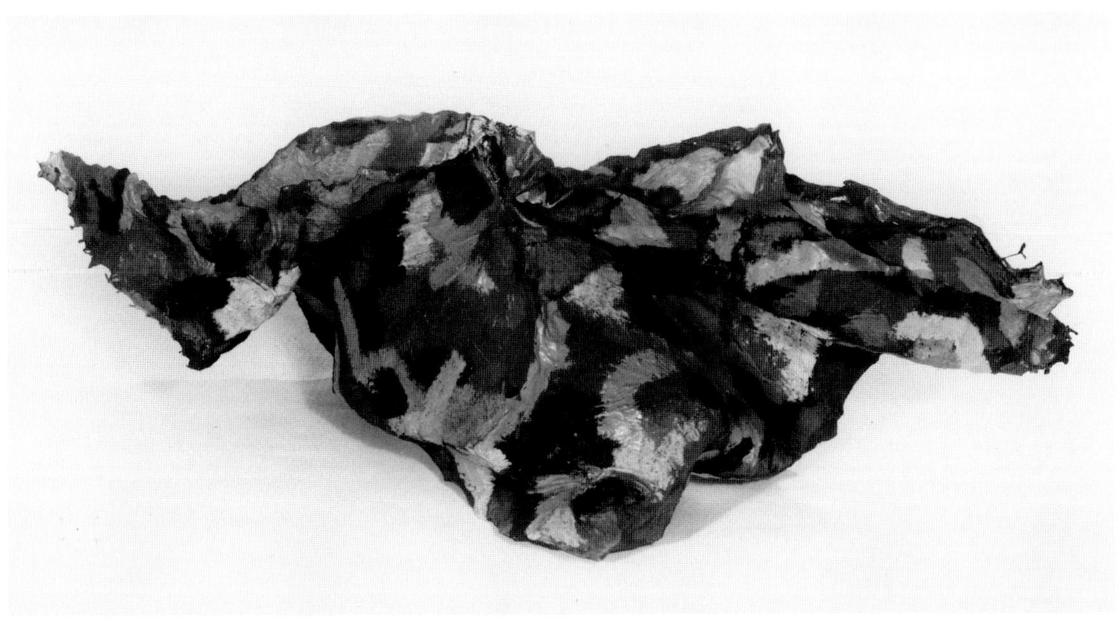

5. *Circular Breathing*, 1981
   oil, casein, and enamel over gessoed fabric
      and wire
   41 × 24 × 23 inches

6. *Remains*, 1982
   oil, casein, and tempera over gessoed fabric
      and wire
   43 × 43 × 52 inches
   illustrated

7. *Becoming Opposites*, 1982
   oil and enamel over gessoed fabric, wire,
      and aluminum
   73 × 45 × 22 inches
   illustrated

8. *Manifest*, 1983
   oil over gessoed fabric, wire, and aluminum
   88 × 51 × 62 inches
   see color plate, frontispiece

9. *Lifeline*, 1984
   oil and enamel over gessoed fabric, wire,
      and aluminum
   79 × 59 × 42 inches
   illustrated

10. *Old Bones*, 1985
    oil over gessoed fabric, wire, and aluminum
    68 × 66 × 34 inches
    see color plate, front cover

11. *A Way Back*, 1985
    oil over gessoed fabric, wire, and aluminum
    53 × 35 × 38 inches
    illustrated

12. *A Child's Memory*, 1985
    oil over gessoed fabric, wire, and aluminum
    90½ × 35 × 28 inches

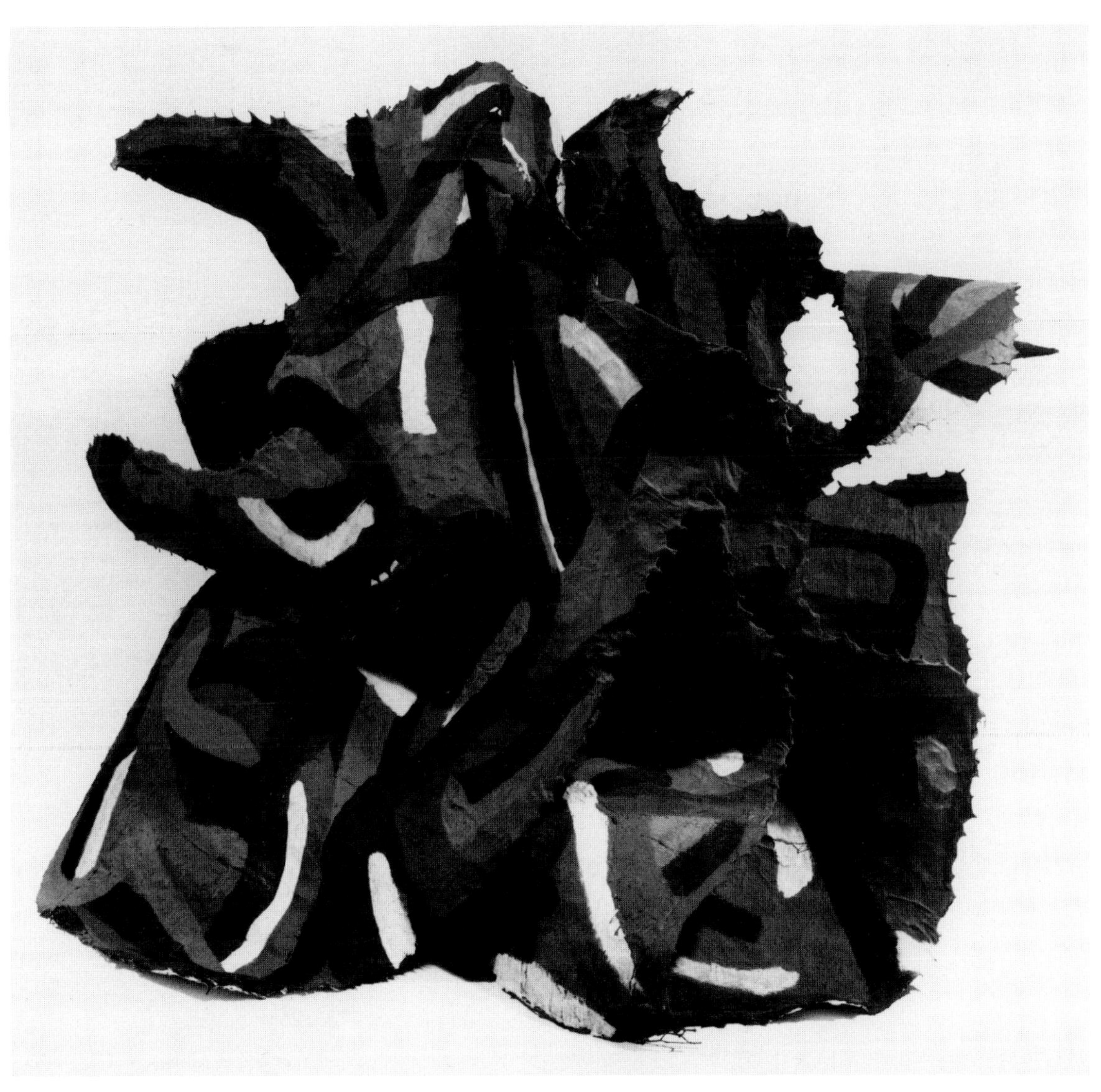

Remains, catalogue no. 6

Becoming Opposites, catalogue no. 7, view A

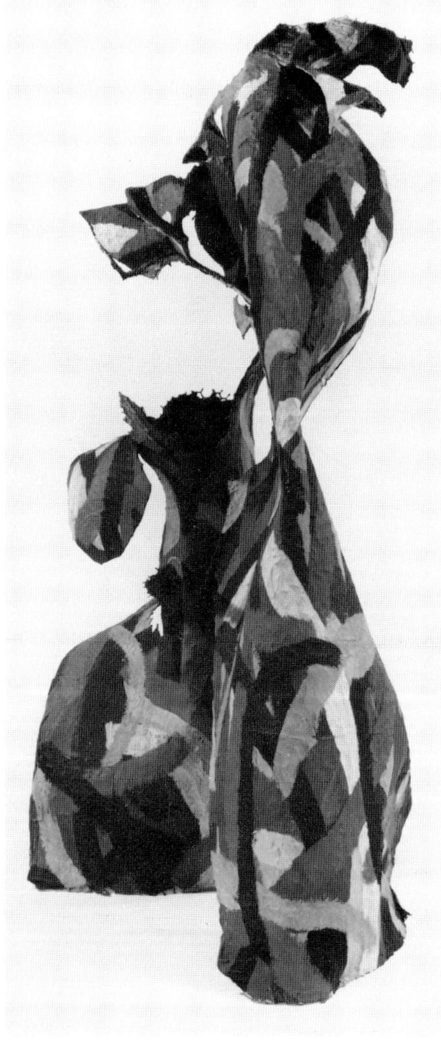

Becoming Opposites, catalogue no. 7, view B

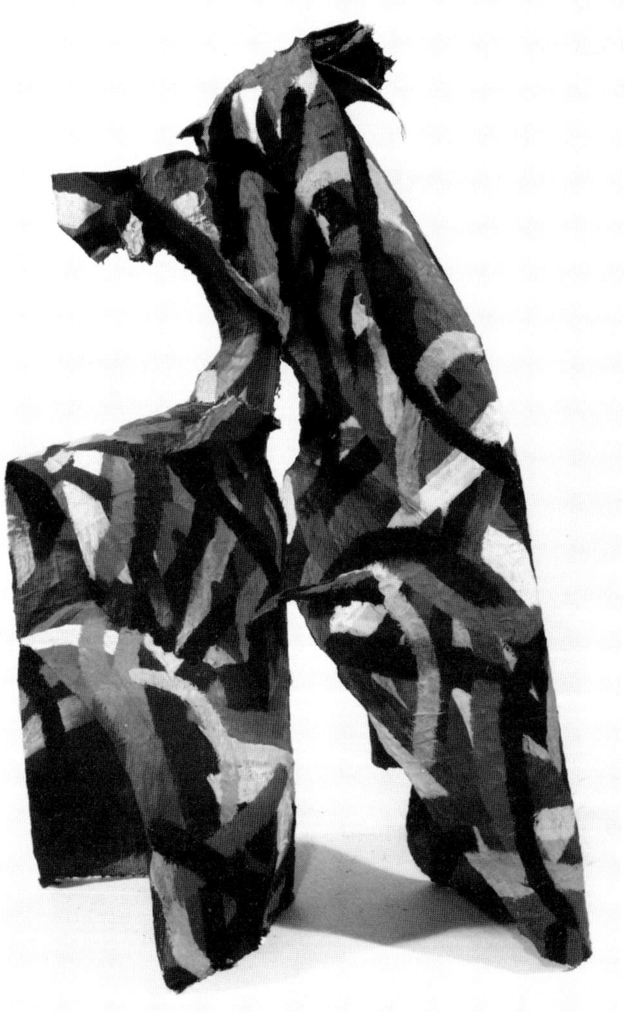

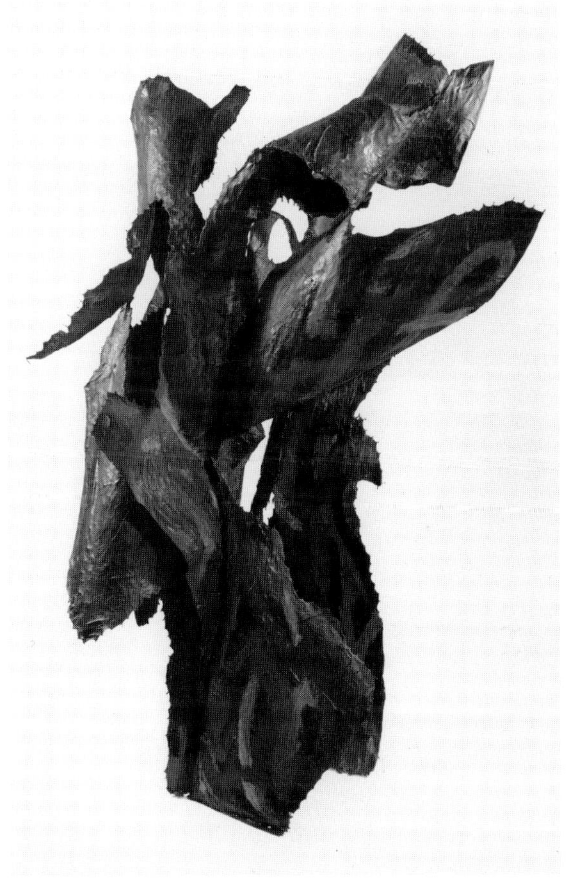

Lifeline, catalogue no. 9, view A

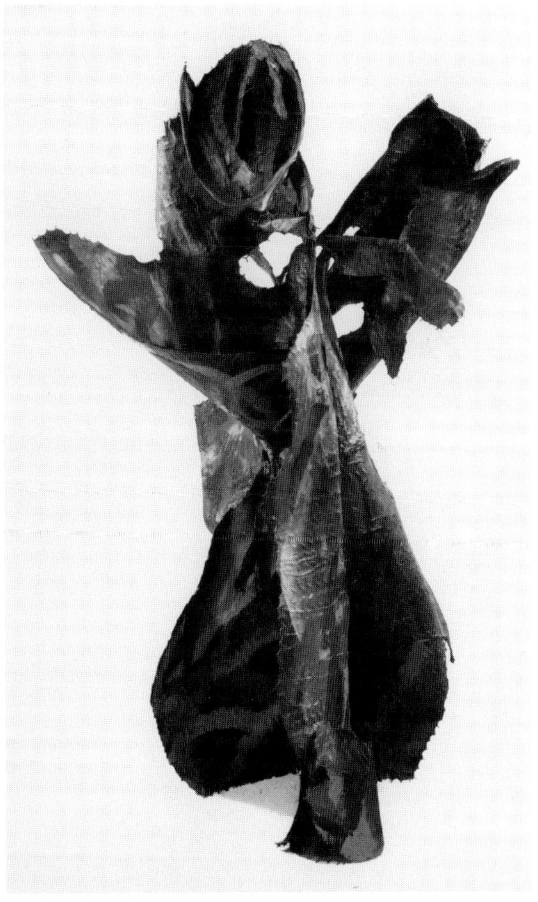

Lifeline, catalogue no. 9, view B

A Way Back, catalogue no. 11

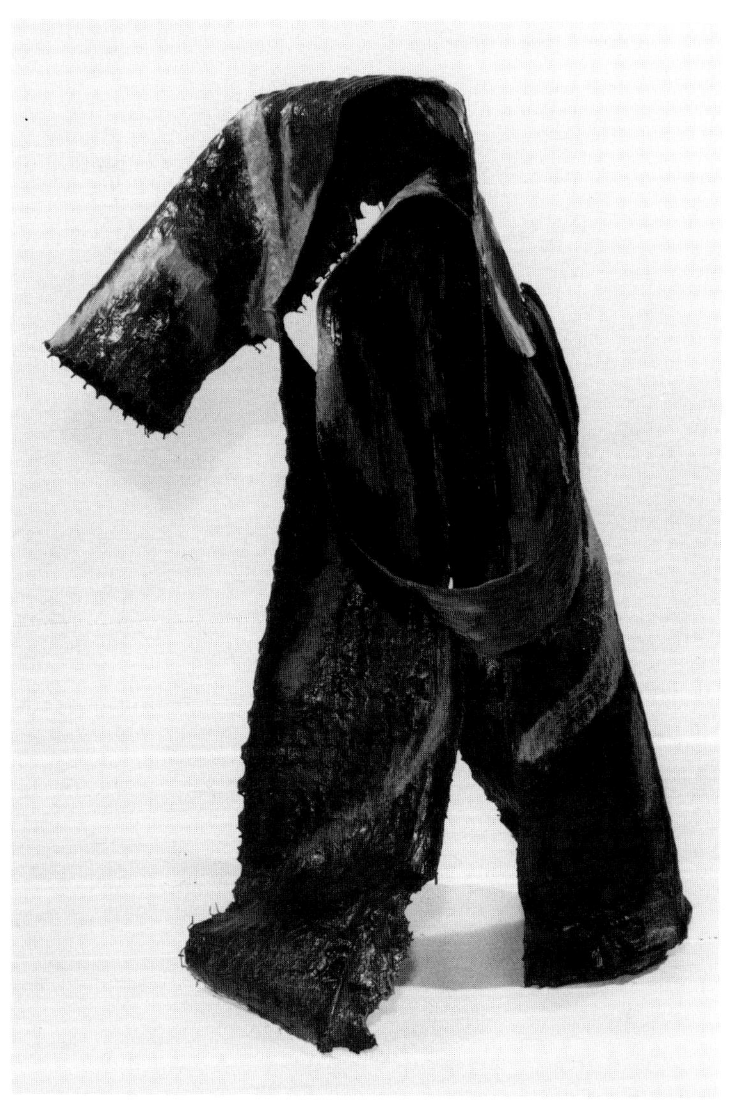